You're about to witness the single greatest change in the way you experience **TIME.** A turning point in human history, but first, we must overcome cognitive dissonance and *two barriers*: the current clock and calendar. You see, you've been living on someone else's time system (Julian & Gregorian Calendar System 46 BC-1582 AD,). A **matrix**, a beginning reality of past civilizations thinking of those times! The single **greatest illusion** and **delusion** of our time!

Everything changes in some way. Even a rock changes over time, but our observation of how we connect daily with clock-time in the 21st century hasn't budged a Planck unit in thousands of years!! We must get ready for the "**Next generation**" time clock, **1440TIME**™!

"To measure is to manage."—Lord Kelvin

"Without a sense of urgency, desire loses its value."—Jim Rohn

Do you want more TIME? Do you want more out of life? Maybe better health? More money? Maybe another leg up in your already excellent career? Smarter? More time with your family?

If you answered yes to any of these questions, then I will show you how a simple mind shift will leave you rich in *TIME*!

©2017 Kevin R. McGrane. All Rights Reserved
ISBN-13:978-0-9836500-1-0
Published by Kevin R. McGrane

Table of Contents

Preface..5
Dear Future Time Master...7
Birth of an Idea...11
Upgrade and Reboot..13
The Clock Matrix..14
What is The 1440 Power System®..........................21
The Time Conversion Table.....................................25
1440TIME™..32
Free-Time..35
The 1440Clock..37
Minute Perspective...38
Zone One - **Sleep**..39
Zone Two - **Livlihood** (work) Zone..........................48
Perception and Perspective.....................................54
Zone Three - **On-Time** Zone (free time) 55
Final Notes..67

Preface

This book explores new concepts that are not widely known. I decided to share this proactive discovery, **1440TIME**™ and **The 1440 Power System**®, with everyone, but it will greatly impact the ones who are self-driven and looking to raise the bar even higher for themselves.

I did not "invent" the concept of a **new time clock**. Instead, I took an "old time" concept in place for thousands of years and **upgraded** the "time component" to the speed of which our modern world runs today. My desire to "be better" and strive for more has led me to transform the old "standard" view of time into the new dynamic and powerful 21st century concept called **1440TIME**™ and the connector-- **The1440 Power System**®. When applied correctly, it will change the way you see, experience, and value time forever.

Please go to my website www.1440time.com to further enhance your "1440TIME™" experience. By exploring my website, you will view, connect, and feel the power of the "**1440 revolution**™" in real-time.

 Enjoy this gift of TIME...
Kevin McGrane

From The Matrix

"You take the blue pill, the story ends. You wake up in your bed and believe whatever you want to believe. You take the red pill, you stay in Wonderland, and I show you how deep the rabbit hole goes."
—Morpheus to Neo

The 1440 Power System®
Think Outside the Clock™

Dear Future Time Masters,

It is with great pleasure that I present to you **The 1440 Power System®/1440TIME™** book. Its secret blend of ingredients will activate and optimize your life, enabling time to flow seamlessly and naturally as the past, present, and future collide to form the only time that matters: this moment **right now.** Now is all we have, and even though it's easy to say and think, it is much harder *to do* and *stay in the now consistently*. We spend so much of our now "thinking" about the "past" and what's to come in our "future." If this is true, are we living and taking in all that the *now really offers*?

The 1440 Power System® was created to help anyone become present, stay present, and live in presence by using a simple but ingenious strategy for even the most unconscious of minds to reconcile with.

1440 TIME™ is the **cornerstone** of this 21st century principle, utilizing a patent 1440 Minute Countdown Clock[1] as the instrument to activate time awareness. This in turn, enables anyone to get and stay present anytime, anywhere at a glance.

---

[1] US Patent Number 9,593,352

We all know how hard it is to stay present. Our modern society has us essentially all connected 24/7 with no days off to recharge the battery and synchronize with our natural time frequency. Our TV, smartphones, tablets, and social media have become our life support to the world as we know it, hanging on to every news reel, photo, video, text, or tweet. Being present today means answering your cell phone on one ring, texting back in less than twenty seconds, and responding to emails within ten minutes. This collective folly seems to be the new normal for today's world, what's yet to come might be even more mind-bending, as the technological revolution is advancing exponentially.

Why not try an equally new advancement and perspective for clock-time that is in alignment with the speed of our modern-day world?

It's a new time awareness system which gives people time to **utilize** and **apply** this great technology of the 21st century, raising the human potential, and not just for convenience and conversation.

As found in **The Time Factor** book, the ancient standard clock has been exposed for what it is: an outdated modus operandi for **those times** still is used for **our times**! And because of this erroneous subconscious program, many suffer from *Times Fault Syndrome™* (TFS) and *other time-related stress disorders,* affecting lives, emotions, and productivity. In addition to those, a subtle yet maybe the most important one is, *"People feel as though time is moving faster and faster as they age!"* Who doesn't think that—except for kids under twenty five or maybe Bernie Madoff?

What makes this book one of a kind, is **The 1440 Power System®** and **1440TIME™**. They bring the concepts from "The Time Factor" alive by seeing the 1,440 minutes we have every day in a declining real-time application. This reinforces and builds upon the theoretical concepts already learned.

You know from The Time Factor Book this is no *ordinary time management system*. Even though many are good, **The 1440 Power System®** brings an *entirely new approach to processing time that's been missed by every book* out there.

Think about it. We have hundreds of books and systems to manage your time, over 1.5 billion Google results on "time management", and thousands of online courses available to learn about almost anything. We have smart phones, email, and text messaging, which should allow us to be more organized and save time—yet most barely have enough time in a day to get the basics or fixed to-do's done, *e.g., sleep, work, appointments, house chores, etc.,* leaving little time to **go for more**. Why is that? The irony is, the more you chase the clock and calendar, the more it controls your life, and the faster time moves by, although perceptional of course.

1440TIME™ is the **premium** or the **Gold standard** time clock for the 21st century. It is a superior upgrade from the *old time standard clock* from thousands of years ago, no longer compatible with the speed of life. Its effect is like the way time feels when we change our clocks back in the fall: We get that **"extra hour"** of time on the clock. We have more time and we're not rushing around in the morning. *Boy, does that illusion of getting twenty-five hours in that day feel good.*

Birth of an Idea

I have a great product to share with you today. Let me tell you a little about the history of how it came about. It was founded on that great motivational igniter that **"sense of urgency"** feeling... do or die, as the clock is running out! The times when we rise above the pressure, the uncertainty, and we get the job done, or that flash of genius hits us. Hence, **1440TIME**™ was born.

What started out in 2007 as a simple change in the way I perceived the clock has now turned into a ten-year adventure into the conceptual world of time. Little did I know that my life would be transformed forever, and that this transformation would result in my authoring two books: *The Time Factor & The 1440Power System®, and finally be able obtain my U.S. Patent Minute Countdown Clock*[1], *which is called 1440TIME*™.

1440TIME™ is a major advancement toward improving human productivity for the 21st century. It is a fascinating breakthrough on how to measure and manage clock-time in the modern world. Is the average person on Main Street ready for this yet? Probably not!

---

[1] US Patent Number 9,593,352

I believe this is the most efficient way to tell, measure, and process time in the world today! Not only does it unlock the inner potential of anyone who is ready to apply the system, but it will also *awaken one's own Time Awareness System™ within.* While this approach may be new and unique, it has universal application to anyone who uses a watch or clock during the day. This slight shift in one's subconscious regarding time will bring powerful, long-lasting results, and can be accomplished instinctually with little or no effort. It's similar to the way a child learns to ride a bike: After just a few run-a-longs, solo pushes, and perhaps a spill or two, instinct takes over, and the child's feet begin to push the pedals unconsciously, then the child learns how to ride a bike. Most importantly, however, *once learned, one cannot "unlearn" how to ride a bike.* In the same sense, once one learns what **1440TIME™** is, how it functions, and how it is applied, it *canno*t be unlearned.

It is time to move past the old standard version of our clock-time reality passed down from centuries ago, to an entirely new and different thought process!

Upgrade and Reboot

The brain's processing speed is enormous. Once you calibrate and reboot your CPU (*brain*) to *1440TIME*™ (*running in fractal minutes*), and remove the outdated **time programs** (*running in hours and days*), your human potential has just been upgraded exponentially! Much like what happens when technology is upgraded today, we can do **more** and in **less time**!

As an added *bonus*, what would you think if I could change your perception of time by an increase of 12,000% a day!? Is it real? Is it possible?

This book's premise is just that. By changing the way we perceive the standard clock and calendar, we can make a *transformational shift* in our lives. This premise is built on the principle that we have been living in the 21st century in a way that is deeply flawed and *out of sync with time as we perceive it today*. Because of this, we must first overcome two barriers or obstacles!

"You never change things by fighting the existing reality. To change something, build a new model that makes the existing model obsolete". —Richard B. Fuller

The Clock Matrix
Barrier #1

```
8 51405 1   2 51405 1   4 61405 9   8 51405 0
5 61415 1   5 01415 2   9 71415 0   5 31415 3
5 61425 7   3 81425 1   6 41425 6   0 71425 1
3 71435 1   9 11435 3   3 01435 3   4 41435 1
3 60004 2   3 60004 7   1 20004 8   9 60004 8
2 30014 7   SYSTEM RESTORED   1 90014 7
0 60024 3   7 50024 1   0 80024 1   7 50024 2
7 90034 7   9 50034 1   7 40034 5   6 30034 2
0 90044 0   7 20044 4   9 40044 9   8 80044 9
7 30054 6   3 50054 5   8 20054 8   0 90054 6
```

The **1440Power System**® focuses on removing the barriers of the **"clock matrix"** that affect one's daily life. The **first** barrier is *standard clock-time*, in particular, the <u>hour folly</u>. **1440TIME™** utilizes the *minutes you have left in a day* and not the current 12/12-hour dichotomy put into place thousands of years ago. The old hour system was predicated on 12 hours of sunlight and 12 hours of darkness (*hence, the hour mindset*). **1440TIME™** is designed around the 1,440 minutes in a day—where each minute is as intrinsically valuable as the next minute. No "automatic shutdowns" in productivity just because it is 6:00 p.m. Rather, 6:00 p.m. translates into 360 valuable minutes left in the day to accomplish multiple tasks such as getting to the gym for a 20-minute workout, getting ahead on tomorrow's economic news reading a chapter of your favorite book, or start that online course you've been pondering about. The new digital age requires a **new time model**. Does one really need *hours* each day to get smarter, healthier, or to even *think* of new ways to make more money in our lives? Of course not! We need just **minutes** per day (*compounded daily*), including the weekends paired with a **dose of purpose** and the **information highway** to unlock the unlimited potential *we all have* today!

1440TIME™ takes the 12/12 repeat clock *out of the equation* and focuses on how many minutes are left in this **date-in-time**. 1440TIME™ is designed to disrupt your current clock-time thinking. This innovation paradigm shift interrupts the current sideways trending pattern that many are in, setting you up for a parabolic time break-through. You will be off to all time-highs, as **time** now becomes plentiful and recognized as the most important commodity you own!!!

"Think outside the clock" —Kevin McGrane

You can see on the 1440TIME™ watch it says **1080** and the standard time is **6:00 a.m.**

There are only two hands: the minute and second. It starts at 1,440 and counts down until 0. The sun rises at 6:00 a.m. and the moon rises at 9:00 p.m. It's currently set for the summer months. The sun and moon are for concept, but closely depict their movements of an earth day EST. **It is the 21st century sun/moon dial.**

The Eastern Standard Time shown here (9:00 p.m.) is an old linear time system, and is the **clock matrix!** In *1440TIME™*, it's **180**. One clock has you **reacting** and **serving**... *Hurry!! Monday Night Football has just started!* The other is **proactive** and **time serves you**... *Great: I have 180 minutes left today before I go to sleep. So I am going to watch the game if it's good, and get a quick 10-minute workout in at halftime. If not, it's guitar time!!*

How does somebody know what they want if they haven't even seen it? —Steve Jobs

The **clock matrix** starts when we're children in school and we've never looked back. *Why would we*? The standard clock needs no explanation. It just is! Just like two plus two equals four, right?

1440TIME™ can expand our human potential. It is for the movers and shakers. Those who want to get the most out of life have goals and want to meet those goals.

A **goal** has a **timeline**! A *beginning and finish date*. Once you start a goal, the countdown for the completion has begun, which plays right into the **1440 countdown construct.** Does that make sense? If you don't get it, or you just find it interesting, you're just not ready yet. If you do... keep on reading...

Barrier # 2

The second barrier to break will be the connection we have with the **calendar**. Humans have been conditioned and trained over centuries to act and feel a certain way about *words* that represent ancient gods, planets, and our moon. *Monday, Tuesday, Wednesday, Thursday, Friday, Saturday, Sunday, weekends, and holidays* are just **words** that have a psychological attachment to them. These words have no real intrinsic value except for the emotional value you have attached to each one, and people have different attachments to these words. For example, Monday (*moons-day*) might mean **sucks** for many, but for entrepreneurs, it might mean **excitement** or **money**.

Friday means payday and happiness for most, but if you're an EMT, Friday might mean a *busy night ahead*. Saturday (Saturn's Day) and Sunday (Sun's Day) are words that have developed meanings of their own. They are now synonymous *for most* with **"off"** days or **"do what I want"** days. In reality, they're just another 1,440 minutes in the day of our lives. **1440TIME™** helps quarantine this word malware. When this happens, awareness and mindfulness surface, and your all around personal productivity will surge by more than **30% a week** and for many more, even higher... **Control the clock control the game!**

Unfortunately, nobody can be told what 1440TIME™is. You have to see it for yourself. You take the blue pill, the story ends; you wake up in your bed and believe whatever you want to believe. Or you take the red pill, you stay in 1440land and I'll show how far down the rabbit hole time really goes!!! Remember, **all I'm offering is the truth, nothing more...** *Follow me...*

The 1440 Power System®
Think Outside the Clock™

What is The 1440 Power System®?

The first thing we must recognize is that 24 hours x 60 minutes = 1,440 minutes. That is, 24 hours are the same as 1,440 minutes in a day. No one receives any more or less *"Equal Opportunity Time" (EOT)*. No matter race, creed, color, or gender, <u>we're all equal</u> and allotted **one daily time-voucher** worth 1,440 minutes to use every day. It's in this voucher where your life unfolds... Enjoy this one... it's on me.

However, we must reformat and recalibrate the brain first to think in terms of minutes all day every day! Not just in the morning, when rushing around to get the kids to school, get to work, or that appointment. The minute system is already partial used every day by tens of millions of people. It's just not been formerly recognized yet, leaving most unaware of this way of thinking all day and every day. In fact, is the very *key to the activation of The 1440 Power System®!*

The current paradigm today is what I call a **"Pavlovian conditioning"** of the clock & calendar. It permeates the mind unconsciously and it should. It is all we have known and been taught up until now, that is...

As Deepak Chopra says so well, when it comes to the way we perceive things today, we are under the "conditioning of social hypnosis."

Are we being herded by our willingness to think about time in a way that serves others, or maybe the powerful of today, i.e., Wall St. and the media? Do the mechanical clock and calendar have you in a trance and you don't even know it—unconsciously compliant and conditioned to ancient names, *i.e., the days in a week* and *numbers on a circular sphere*, to respond, think, and feel certain ways based on what time it is or day it is!?

Greek mythology gave us Chronos, *the god of time*, today known as chronological time or linear time. The Romans gave us June from Juno an ancient goddess, July and August for Julius and Augustus Caesar, March from Mars, the ancient god of war, January from Janus the god of opening and closing doors, and Saturday from the God Saturn. The Northern Germanic tribes gave us the Norse Gods for Tuesday, Wednesday, Friday and well-known Thor, the god of thunder, for Thursday. In Latin, September means "seven," but September is our calendar's ninth month, October is from the Latin *octo* which means "eight," but October is our calendar's tenth month. Furthermore, our seven-day week comes from the seven most visible planets to man: The Sun, Moon, Mercury, Venus, Mars, Saturn, and Jupiter. They are just ancient beliefs and **words** from a *time long past.* Systems created and changed over the years by the *ancient and powerful* of the moment to quantify time, likely implemented to control the masses and make sure they paid their taxes and debt on time.

You must unlearn what you have learned— Yoda

The 1440 Power System® alters the ancient way of thinking about time. Every day is just **"1440 minutes"** and is that not true? Think about it. How do you feel and think about the word Saturday versus Tuesday? Is Saturday just another 1,440 minutes in a day of our lives (and fifty two of them at that), or is it "groundhog's day", a reoccurring "free" day word named after planet Saturn?

It's 10:10A.M. Do you know what time it is?

Thor's Day, Julius 13th 2017

On the next page, you will see a *Time Conversion Table,* allowing you to see this new measurement of time, further helping in the time adjustment process. *Remember: What we focus on expands* and *clarity is power.* You will know when it's starting to work as time will expand and awareness intensifies, and as many friends of mine have said, "Kevin, it feels like I have more time now," confirming what I've already known.

Time Conversion Table			
1 year	=	525,600	minutes
1 Quarter (avg)	=	131,400	minutes
1 month (avg)	=	43,800	minutes
1 week	=	10,080	minutes
1 day	=	1,440	minutes
1 hour	=	60	minutes

The conversion table expands stretches and extends time out. A year is no longer seen as just another year. It becomes 525,600 minutes long, hosting a measurable timeline—counting down by 1,440 minutes every day. The quarter now becomes 131,400 minutes long. The month becomes 43,800 minutes. The week becomes 10,080 minutes long. The day becomes *1,440* minutes and finally, to the present moment, the seconds and minutes, the NOW that makes up the days, weeks, months, and years left on **Bertrand Planes Life Clock** here in the natural world.

Measure it or wing it. —Unknown

1440TIME™ delivers a *small daily dose* of **"sense urgency"** that helps us "recognize it," making it more valuable. Time now becomes **"tangible"** whether it is working out, reading books, studying, taking care of kids, commuting to work, home chores, getting to the mall on a Saturday, or just watching TV. Our brain now immediately goes to work and soon activates the **Reticular Activating System (RAS)**. Think of the RAS as the gatekeeper, sifting through the copious amounts of information the brain encounters daily, trying to figure out which information is significant enough to let through or be pushed aside like spam. The RAS, in turn will assist in the activation of the Time Awareness System™ **(TAS)**: *a powerful inner awareness* of the *NOW* as time itself begins to awaken. The new default (*minutes*) becomes the conscious program of the mind, replacing the outdated clock & calendar as you currently know it, *i.e., (hours, days, and months)*. The brain now processes things faster, in "minutes" or even "seconds" needed to get a task done, yet you're not hurried. This leaves the standard clock and a few mythical gods like "Horus", "Chronos", "Juno", "Thor", Saturn, and "Janus" behind where they belong.

The standard clock and the calendar have most running around like our rabbit friend below.

Never having enough and always craving more. Sure, most process by the minute in the morning rush, at lunchtime, and many other times, but it doesn't last. We fade back to the **default clock,** *the ancient twelve-hour standard time clock* once again, back to the Pavlovian clock of the past. You see, you can always do more in sixty minutes than in one hour, and even more in one hundred and twenty minutes than in two hours. Try it for yourself. It is all a matter of perception and perception is reality.

We apprehend time by making motion. —Aristotle

Time has been blamed for all sorts of things, from why we failed the class, to not having time for exercise, practicing, reading, cooking, making engagements, marriage, friendships, and even for paying our bills. This is what 's called **Time's Fault Syndrome** (TFS), the automatic default excuse for blaming time for why we couldn't do something consciously or subconsciously. The great news is once we eliminate the clock as the reason why we can't do something, we are forced to own-up and answer accordingly, and that is exactly what **1440TIME™** does. You'll now have to say to yourself regardless, *"I have the time, but do I really want it bad enough?"* Regardless of whether it's getting to the gym, running around the block, taking that class, or learning about finances. Time as the ally for creating the results you want or time as the reasons and blame for why you can't or don't!

1440TIME™ doesn't make you rich, get you that great body, take the classes, or read the books for you, but it *does* give you the *time* to do any of them!

Accusing the Times is but excusing ourselves.
—Thomas Fuller

What does 525,600-minutes look like in a year and how many of those minutes are in the **free minute zone,** (*when not working or sleeping*)?

Example:

Work-Week:

1. **Free minutes in normal work week = 2,100**

    After using:
    - 7 hours for sleep
    - 10 hours for work

Leaving seven hours of free time daily

- ✓ (7x60) = 420(5 days) = 2100

Weekends OFF:

2. **Free minutes on weekends = 1,920**

    After using:
    - 8 hours for sleep
    - 16 hours awake: (16 x 60x 2 = 1,920)

    2,100 + 1,920(52 weeks) **= 209,000**

Total free minutes an average person has in one year equals 209,000 or 145 days! Wow, that's a lot of time...

The clock has decided to take time into its own hands.

— Anonymous

The **1,440 Power System**® is broken into **three zones**:
- **Sleep** (most important)
- **Work** (now called **Livelihood**)
- **Free time** (now called **On-Time**)

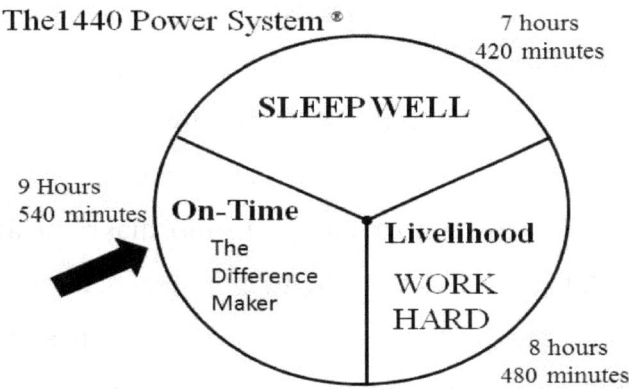

On-Time is where you make it happen. It separates the contenders from the pretenders. This is where PowerTime (PT) and PowerTime Plus (PTP) shine and *go to work for you*. We don't say **free time** anymore as we know what happens when we get things for free. That's why so many *unconsciously* seem to waste this powerful energy zone of the day on many un-powering pursuits and thoughts. After all, it is *free time...*

For every minute spent in organizing, an hour is earned. — Harvey MacKay Quotes

When time is broken down this way, it becomes a potent ally. When *sleeping*, sleep well. When *working*, work hard. When you're **On-Time**, your brain knows it is the difference maker". This is where *success/ dreams are made and fulfillment manifests itself.*

PTP time is where goals become a reality, flab becomes fitness, and mindlessness becomes mindfulness. For many, On-Time is *autonomic*, unknowingly being controlled by a primordial clock and calendar. Although this time might be realized, it has yet to be recognized for its true potential. With the use of 1440TIME™ and Power System, you will be able to increase your personal productivity and avoid the overused excuse of blaming "time". By splitting the 1,440 minutes up, it simplifies and breaks down time into *three distinct components for* the brain to process: **Sleep, Livelihood and On-Time.** Whatever zone you're in, your brain automatically goes there! Sleeping is for sleep. Livelihood is your means of support. On-Time is for life's maintenance, fun, relaxing and for *going for more.*

Awareness without action is worthless. —Dr. Phil

1440TIME™

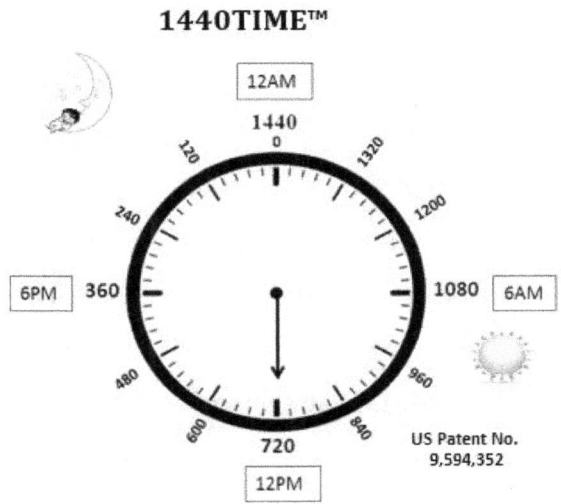

1440 Minute Countdown Clock[1] works with the Sun's movement of the day. Think of the how the Cowboys and farmers of the past worked their day *Sunup to Sundown*. The Sun was their clock and they worked along with it. *"Boys, we're burning daylight,"* as John Wayne said in *The Cowboys* in 1972. The 1440TIME™ clock replaces the Sun, working much in the same way, except it covers **one entire day of time**. We have light, electricity, and the internet today, so we can work after the sun goes down with no problem, unlike the first two million years humans were on this earth.

---

[1] US Patent Number 9,593,352

The 1440 Power System® quantifies time and breaks it into three distinct ZONES, giving you the big picture (*one day in time*), yet driving home the relevance of each of its individual parts. Every day is just another 1,440 minutes—**sunup to the moon down**, and another fresh chance to play in this game of *life*. A new day to create, to love, and to laugh more —a new day to work, to enjoy, to learn, and to appreciate that each day is unique, for once it's gone, it is retired to the record books forever.

We get only one ticket into this great game called life on earth and receive one daily time-voucher, good for 1,440 minutes with no rollover minutes granted. If we can't find passion and purpose in those facts, then it's just not your time yet.

Warning: Just knowing how to divide your time up isn't enough. In order to do so, you *must take ownership* of your 1,440 minutes every day.

The simple joy of living between the sunrises was gone. —From *The Timekeeper* by Mitch Albom

1440TIME™

What is the first thing people see when they get up every morning ? Yes, the clock... When you wake up, you see 6:00 a.m. With 1440TIME™, you'll see 1080...! *There is a difference.* The outdated standard clock has you on automatic pilot, a *"Pavlovian conditioning"*, trained to think and act not only by numbers on a clock, but ancient names for days of a week: *Monday, Tuesday, Wednesday, Thursday, Friday, Saturday, and Sunday.* Now, it even controls the way you feel and act subconsciously about a particular day of the week. Don't you just hate "Mondays," or should we say Moon's Day?

Let's look at the word Free-Time?

In the world of time, there is no such thing *as* **free-time.** You might be home from work and might be off on what's called a Saturday or Sunday, but time is **never off,** either. Think of a light switch. The switch may be off, but the electricity is still on and active. Since we think and say **FREE-TIME** when not working or taking care of the kids, we self-sabotage ourselves subconsciously. Think about it! When you get something for **free,** does it carry the same weight as if you had to earn it and pay for it with your time, effort, and money? NO…! So free-time is now called **ON-TIME!** In addition, we say things like, *"What are you doing when you're off work,"* or *"Today, I am off."* Instead of off-time, or off from work, we say, **"on-time."** Work is a job for most. It's a means of support, "livelihood." **Off-time applies what? "You're not working?"** Like a light switch, even though it's off, the electricity is still active and **on** behind the scenes. So when you're done with work, we should be saying *"What are you doing when you're on time?", or "Today I am on time."* Or just, *"What are you doing later when you're* **on***?"* Off implies you're off from your job, but that's when you should be **turning ON!** This is when you live, when you have control, when you can think, dream, plan, and do on your terms. If you work hard at your job for someone or some company every day then why can't you work just as hard for yourself when you're *on your time*? You're not off from work. You're **ON-TIME** now. This is where and when life truly unfolds for most **who want more out of their lives.** On-Time is that time when not **sleeping** or **working** *and* called the <u>difference maker</u> in The 1440 Power System®. It is also where **Power Time and Power Time Plus** reside, which we'll go over in more detail on the coming pages. For now, remember that *time is never free*! You might be off from work or your job, but the clock of life is always ticking. *There are no roll-over minutes in the world of time too bad, right?*

There's time enough, but none to spare.
—Charles W. Chesnutt

1440TIME™ is an innovation paradigm shift. It breaks the old pattern of the way we get up in the morning. Even though you know it's Monday, you'll see **1080** on the 1440TIME™ morning clock. It takes on a different feel, believe me. I've been waking up to 1020 for about five years now and still have gratitude every morning for those minutes given to me, and use them wisely. **1440TIME™** will work best for those who have goals or are shooting for something they want to finish. Many already use some sort of timer. *Countdown timers* encourage focus; teach us to value our time, and help us measure how much we can accomplish in a quick period. Also, when seen this way, a slight *sense of urgency* is created and is a good thing. Think about how many times you've gotten the job done when a sense of urgency was applied. Think about the people who rose above and beyond what they thought was possible when an extreme sense of urgency was put on them? Whether it's an athlete in the last seconds of a game, or a fireman saving a life in a burning building.

"I live my life with a sense of urgency that most people can't comprehend." —Marc Bolan

Minute Perspective

The 1440 Minute System			
1 year	=	525,600	minutes
1 Quarter (avg)	=	131,400	minutes
1 month (avg)	=	43,800	minutes
1 week	=	10,080	minutes
1 day	=	1,440	minutes
1 hour	=	60	minutes

The total approximate **free minutes** for the average American in one year equals 209,000 or 145 days. The three events below total about **100,000 minutes:**

- **162 baseball games** *(150 mins a game **24,300**)*
- **833 reruns of Seinfeld** *(30 mins a show **24,999**)*
- **A four-year bachelor's degree** *(40 courses @ 14 weeks @ 90 minutes a class **50,400**)*

You never looked at time this way, huh? It is amazing how people actually spend so much of their time!

It's what you do in your free time that will set you free—or enslave you. — Jarod Kintz

1. SLEEP-ZONE

Sleep is the best meditation.
—Dalai Lama

Sleep is the most important zone of The 1440 Power System®. Without good sleep, the remaining zones will suffer daily and dramatically more over time.

Our body needs sleep to repair itself on the cellular level to be able to function at full capacity during waking energy hours, whether it's in our livelihood zone or in our OT zone. So many people aren't sleeping well and wonder why their lives lack energy and passion. If we don't sleep well, we wake up groggy, grouchy, lethargic and uninspired. Our day starts on edge as the traffic gets on our nerves. At work, it's tough to give our best, so we settle for mediocrity. The day is finally over and we head home—it's our "**free time**" now, but do we have the energy and drive to excel in this zone (*the difference maker*), or just enough to get by, hoping the weekend gets here soon? *Sleep well and sleep peacefully.*

Look at the 1440 Power System® again below. I am using seven hours for sleep, ten hours for work, and seven hours for **On-Time**. In this scenario, you would have 420 minutes to use for whatever— now invest just ten percent (42 minutes) just three days a week into PTP for **fitness, education, or some extra income pursuits** and multiply that by fifty two weeks, and you're over **6,500 total minutes in a year**. That's enough to make some real difference and impact in your life.

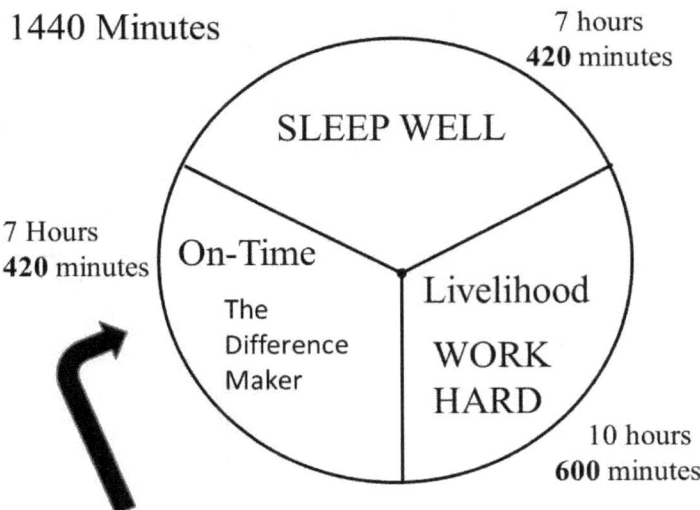

The price of anything is the amount of life you exchange for it. — Henry David Thoreau

The 1440 Power System® applies the breakdown method. Breaking things down into smaller units or chunks is a strategy that many professionals implement. It works, so why not use this same winning formula for our everyday lives? Look at the Power System in action using the example from the last page.

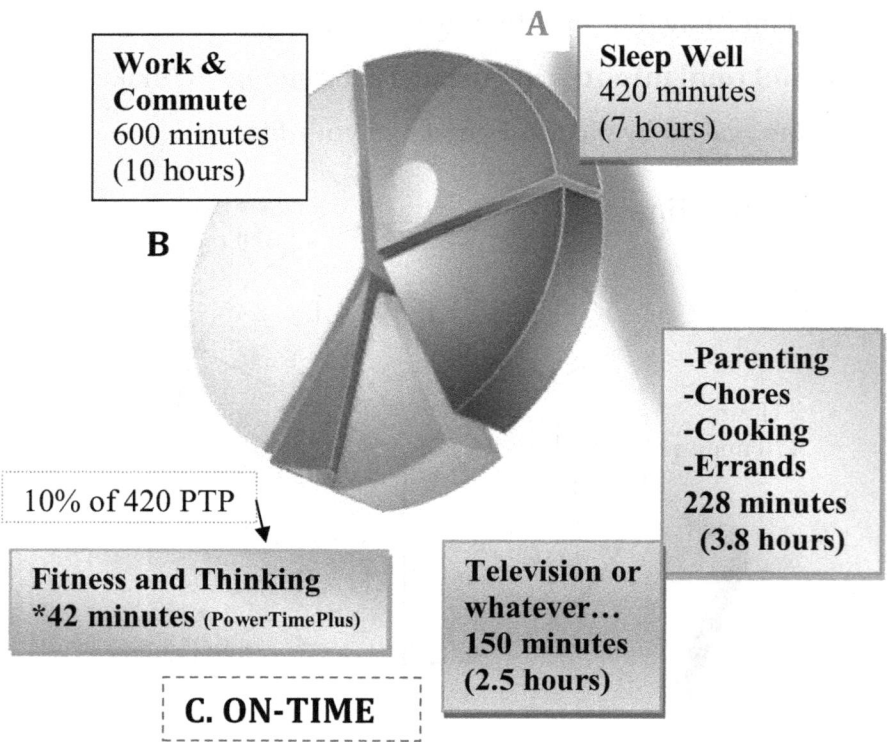

A

Sleep Well
420 minutes
(7 hours)

Work & Commute
600 minutes
(10 hours)

B

-Parenting
-Chores
-Cooking
-Errands
228 minutes
(3.8 hours)

10% of 420 PTP

Fitness and Thinking
*42 minutes (PowerTimePlus)

Television or whatever…
150 minutes
(2.5 hours)

C. ON-TIME

Sleep Time 420 minutes/Waking Time 1020 minutes

Seeing time and breaking it down this way will activate your **Time Awareness System™ (TAS)**. Once activated, it remains activated. TAS works in unison with the Reticular Activating System (*RAS*), the part of the brain that acts as a *gatekeeper*, determining what information gets in and out. Once your TAS is activated, once the gatekeeper (RAS) puts time on **high alert**, time itself becomes a powerful conscious tool. Now that your brain has accepted The 1440 Power System®, **everything** gets processed by some *time-weighted factor*, e.g., your job, parenting, chores, the television you watch, social media, the books and magazines you read, the movies you see, the number of innings you watch a baseball game, even the time you spend with others will be processed in some *time-weighted factor* now. Hence, the Time Value of Time concept is alive and well.

In my book **The Time Factor,** the *Time Value of Time* applies the same concept the time value of money has in finance.(More on this later in the Book.) **Nevertheless, none of this will matter unless we SLEEP WELL!!!!** The next few pages are resources I found to help reinforce the importance of sleep, and a few techniques to help you sleep from Dr. Oz.

Why is Sleep Important?

Missing even 90 minutes of sleep for just 1 night can reduce your daytime alertness by as much as 32%. That's enough to impair your memory and your thinking ability—your safety on the job and on the road. The National Sleep Foundation's 2009 poll showed that as many as 1.9 million drivers have had a car crash or a near miss due to drowsiness in the past year. Here are a few more reasons snoozing is important for your health:

- **It maintains a strong immune system.** Sleep deprivation compromises immune function and makes you more vulnerable to disease.
- **It slows aging.** Too little sleep elevates levels of stress hormones and lowers levels of growth hormone, necessary for cell repair.
- **It prevents diabetes.** Sleeplessness increases insulin resistance, a precursor to type 2 diabetes.
- **It keeps you slim.** When you're sleep deprived, you have more of the appetite-stimulating hormone, ghrelin, in your blood and less appetite-curbing leptin, a combo that leaves you longing for junk food.
- **It can make you happier.** Insomniacs face a higher risk of depression, alcoholism, and suicide.

Source: http://www.prevention.com/health/health-concerns/sleep-center/why-sleep-so-important

Importance of Sleep: Six reasons not to scrimp on sleep

A report from Harvard's Women's Health Watch.

A survey found that more people are sleeping less than six hours a night, and sleep difficulties visit 75% of us at least a few nights per week. A short-lived bout of insomnia is generally nothing to worry about. The bigger concern is chronic sleep loss, which can contribute to health problems such as weight gain, high blood pressure, and a decrease in the immune system's power.

They also suggest six reasons to get enough sleep:

1. Learning and memory: Sleep helps the brain commit new information to memory through a process called memory consolidation. In studies, people who'd slept after learning a task did better on tests later.
2. Metabolism and weight: Chronic sleep deprivation may cause weight gain by affecting the way our bodies process and store carbohydrates, and by altering levels of hormones that affect our appetite.
3. Safety: Sleep debt contributes to a greater tendency to fall asleep during the daytime. These lapses may cause falls and mistakes such as medical errors, air traffic mishaps, and road accidents.

4. Mood: Sleep loss may result in irritability, impatience, inability to concentrate, and moodiness. Too little sleep can also leave you too tired to do the things you like to do.
5. Cardiovascular health: Serious sleep disorders have been linked to hypertension, increased stress hormone levels, and irregular heartbeat.
6. Disease: Sleep deprivation alters immune function, including the activity of the body's killer cells. Keeping up with sleep may also help fight cancer.

Source: http://www.health.harvard.edu/press_releases/8-tips-to-a-good-nights-sleep-without-medicine-from-the-harvard-womens-health-watch

Lack of sleep

Sleep is restorative and improves not only memory, recall, and learning, but also the body's physical health. Studies have shown that "beauty sleep" is real (you look more attractive after a good night's rest), and it also keeps the body's level of ghrelin, the "hunger hormone," low, allowing natural weight control, which, of course, supports health and good food choices.

http://living.msn.com/style-beauty/makeup-skin-care-hair-tips/10-surprising-things-that-are-aging-you-1#7

"You know you're in love when you can't sleep because reality is finally better than your dreams." — *Dr. Seuss*

Deep Sleep Now By Dr. Oz and Dr. Michael Roizen

5 Ways to Set the Mood for Sleep

1. **A Cool, Dark Room**
   Get the zzz's you deserve. The temperature and darkness is a signal to the pineal gland to kick up melatonin production and knock you out.
2. **No Laptops. No TV.**
   Ideally, the bed is used for two things and two things only. If you have any other type of stimuli like work or a TV, you're not sending your body the right message that it's time for sleep. Need more incentive. People who don't have a TV in the bedroom have 50 percent more sex than those who do.
3. **Add White Noise**
   Use a fan for background noise. That, or get one of those machines that let you pick sounds from the rainforest to the ocean. This drowns out the couple fighting next door and the drag races outside so your subconscious stays pristine as you count sheep.
4. **Dress Appropriately**
   The best clothing should be non-restricting and non-allergenic (both the fabric and how it's washed).
5. **Establish a Standard Wake-up Time**
   This includes weekends! This helps reset your circadian rhythm and trains you to stay on schedule if your rhythms happen to wander, like during traveling.

Source: http://www.oprah.com/health/Deep-Sleep-Now-Staying-Young/1

Lack of sleep costing US economy up to $411 billion per year

- Lower productivity levels and the higher risk of mortality resulting from sleep deprivation have a significant effect on a nation's economy.
- Sleep deprivation increases the risk of mortality by 13 per cent and leads to the U.S. losing around 1.2 million working days a year.
- Increasing nightly sleep from under six hours to between six and seven hours could add $226.4 billion to the U.S. economy.

https://www.eurekalert.org/pub_releases/2016-11/rc-los112816.php

We are finished with the most important zone of the day, **sleep**. Without good sleep, our motivational juices will be compromised in our Livelihood and On-Time zones. It is a human function that can't go unrecognized, or sooner or later, you will feel the effects.

Think in the morning. Act in the noon. Eat in the evening. Sleep in the night. — William Blake

2. LIVELIHOOD (Work) – ZONE

When you play, play hard; when you work, don't play at all. — Theodore Roosevelt

Someone recently asked me what I do for a living. Instead of responding the way 99.9 percent of the population would (with a job description) I said, "I sleep for 420 minutes and get up at 6:00 a.m. with a cup of coffee. I turn on the computer, write or read until about 7:00, then visit my basement to work out. By 8:00, I've made breakfast for my family (*most days*) and have taken a shower." When I stopped to catch my breath, the questioner interjected, "*Stop*! That's not what I meant. What do you do to pay your bills? You know, your *job*!" "Oh," I said, "I have a tax preparation company and I help people with finances." How do *you* define your life—**by what you do for a living?** I am an electrician. I am a network specialist. I am a house painter. I work at Home Depot. I am a secretary. I am a doctor. These are all job descriptions, surely, but really, they are nothing more than default answers that define what we do as a means of support. Is this subconscious default program defining our lives by the job we have?

Do you remember Pavlov's dog?

Recently I watched a "protocol expert" on television. This authority on etiquette described the correct way to greet someone: Start with the handshake and some small talk. "Hi, my name's Kevin. What's your name?" (Bill) "Nice to meet you, Bill. What do you do for a living?" Even the experts have decided this is what we're supposed to say. The word **"living"** (as defined by Merriam-Webster) is *"a condition of being alive; full of life and vigor; having a life; to have a life rich in experience."* The dictionary does not say, "Living: real estate agent, or left tackle for the New York Giants." So the next time someone asks you, "What do you do for a living?" you might say, *"Oh, you mean what is my job?"*

The 1440 Power System® breaks down the day using this three-zone strategy to keep you focused on that *zone only.* And when applied daily, awareness in each zone becomes heightened, hence, more efficient and present.

For most of us, work amounts to about one-third of The 1440 Power System®. We work to buy food, clothing, and put a roof over our heads. All for the amenities, safety, and privilege to live in this country. *Do we appreciate and acknowledge this third of our day enough, or does some embedded program have us going through the motions of work-life?* Those whose work is what they love and figure out a way to make it their livelihood, have combined **On-Time** with their **Livelihood**, a powerful blend that leads to sparkling results, *e.g., making more money, being happier, and living their life richer in experience.* For many others, however, their work (*livelihood*) is just a **job**, and when not there, they slip unconsciously into the **free-time zone**, those priceless minutes when not *working or sleeping*. But "**free-time**" is an oxymoron, much like butthead! You may be free from work-time, but there is no *free-time* allotted on the *Game Clock of Life*. And speaking of jobs, the old hourly wage is no more than an adjunct to our outdated clock and calendar. Moreover, even though many companies like Apple and Google are constantly reinventing their work environments to promote vision and creativity among their employees, the majority of employees are paid by the hour with few incentives to go for more each day. *Clock in, clock out...*

I worked for a painting company for over five months while doing research for this book. There were certainly no incentives provided, outside of the fact you got paid every Friday. *Shut up and do your JOB!*

Is the daily grind and robot thinking what it's all about? How about getting paid for the value we bring to sixty minutes, or output per hour, not just for punching an employee time clock? Yeah right, Kevin...

I know a plumber who works at a university. He has mastered the art of *killing time*. He knows what work must be done for the day and exactly how long it will take. Since he is paid by the hour, he has little reason to make any more effort than needed. I also have tax clients who received unemployment income for over a year. When I asked them what they had done with all of that free-time, most said, "nothing". "Nothing". I said, "You had over 350,000 free minutes (*240 days*) and you did nothing with all that time!"

When are we going to break out of our everyday habits? Maybe the current economic backdrop in America will be the needed jolt to work with more focus, intensity, and gratitude for the job we now hold. For those people who take their jobs seriously and use their work time to produce maximum results, there is no such thing as *"killing time."* In addition, if you're self-employed, I guarantee you don't have time to kill. You learned early on that you had to make time your ally, manage it properly, or lose money. Perhaps without knowing it, you're utilizing The 1440 Power System® already. If that's the case, this is just the preverbal icing on the cake for you. However, if you work by the hour in a job with no incentive to go for more, you're still burning through one-third of your day, and can still appreciate and make effective use of this **time** while here. After all, <u>*it's your livelihood.*</u> Work as hard as you can. Raise the level of your game, get noticed, and good things are bound to happen to you.

Your days are each comprised of 1,440 minutes, divided into three zones to accommodate sleep, work, and everything else. If you are *serious* about creating more in your life, this where it begins.

As humans, we all must **sleep**. We all should **work** (in one capacity or another) and we all have **one-third** of our day when we're not, called "free-time", known as **On-Time** in The 1440 Power System®, also the *difference maker*. It is where **PT** and **PTP** reside. So if we want to go for more physically, mentally, and monetarily, this is where it takes place. PERIOD!

This next and final chapter is **On-Time**: a powerful time of the day where the *playmakers shine*. They understand the meaning of **earned success**. This time separates the contenders from the pretenders, the producers from the consumers, and the winners from the nonwinners. By the time you're done with this book, you'll realize your **job** is just part of The 1440 Power System®—it pays for the ticket into the game. The other one-third is for sleep (*repairing of cells, body, and mind*) and the final third, **On-Time,** is for DOING AND GOING FOR MORE...If not, that's okay, too, but no complaining.

Only in our dreams are we free. The rest of the time we need wages. — Terry Pratchett

Perception and Perspective

You're not **off** work. You're **ON-TIME…(OT)**
Hey, so what are you doing later when you're off work?
I don't know, I have lots of stuff to do, but most likely chill, have some dinner, maybe watch some TV, or the game. Sound familiar? Or maybe I have to cook some dinner, do some laundry, and then I am vegging out on the couch with a glass of wine with America's Got Talent. Is it just a play on words? I don't think so! *Off of work*, maybe, but you're never **off the clock**! You're *on your OWN TIME* after work. **SO OWN IT AND CLAIM IT!**

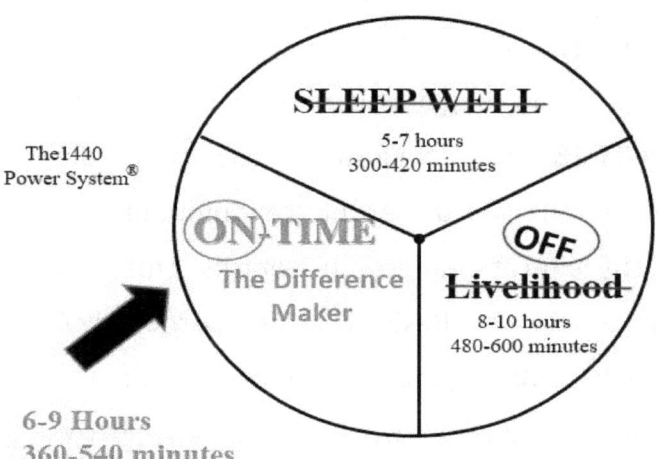

There is a conditioned response associated with the word **OFF** and a conditioned response to the word **ON**. True?

3. ON-TIME (free)-ZONE

Work harder on yourself than you do on your job.

— Jim Rohn

Here we are, the final zone of The 1440 Power System®. You already know that sleep is the most important zone of the day. If we don't sleep well, your **OT** zone will suffer for sure. We also know we need a Livelihood (*a job*) to make money, pay bills, and be responsible for doing our share in America today.

ON-TIME (formerly known as free time) is the *difference maker* for those who want more in their lives physically, educationally, or monetarily. This is where you make it happen. Besides weekends, the only *On-Time* we have during the work week is the time commuting to and from work, and that time between when we get home until we fall asleep. *That's it*...! Your ON-TIME starts here. This is time for chores, performing life's maintenance, enjoying family, and watching TV and movies. We listen to music, go to concerts, the beach, and visit the ballpark, use Facebook, and watch YouTube here. With all that said, if you want a healthier body, a smarter mind, or want a shot at making more money now or sometime in the future, <u>you have to utilize *some* of this time to accomplish that.</u>

On-Time zone consists on the average between 300-480 minutes (*five-eight hours*) for most *weekdays.* This is where **PowerTime Plus** shines and blows away the ancient 12-hour standard clock paradigm. What are **PowerTime** PT and **PowerTime Plus** PTP? Both PowerTime and PowerTime Plus are in The 1440 Power System® inside On-Time. The difference being *PowerTime Plus* is used for goals, dreams, or any defined purpose such as losing weight, writing a book, taking a course, working on those CE credits, studying for an exam, or any other goal or quest that has a *timeline attached to it*. It could be for any predetermined goal that you have set—*no matter what that goal is*, or any worthy ideal you're striving for. **PowerTime** is like **PTP,** but not as acute. You're fully present and aware, and even focused, but the focus is less intensified, yet still present in the now and mindful of time.

Look at the 1440Clock™ below using 300 minutes for **OT** that is when you're off of work and not sleeping. **PT** *will be used all the time in* **OT** *eventually* as your TAS becomes fully engaged. But for now, use PT to get things done efficiently and effectively in the least amount of time, *e.g. chores, food shopping or home projects*, or when have doctor's appointment, you'd know where and when. You'd get there on time, do what you must do, then be done and on your way to whatever is next, even if that's watching TV on the couch. And if you get caught waiting in the doctor's office because they're running late, "*No way;*"... you'll take out your Kindle, read some good material, or answer your emails while waiting patiently.

Where ever you are, is where you're supposed to be.

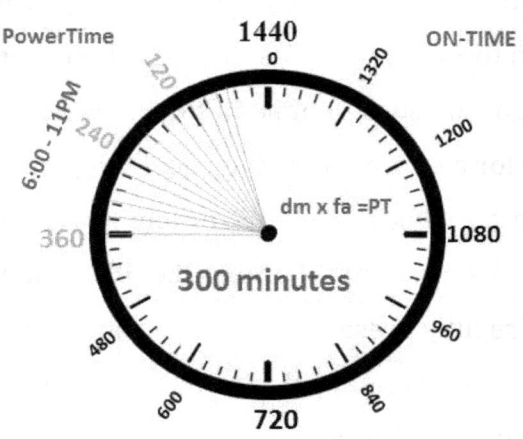

PowerTime Plus is used for goals, no matter how big or small. The catch is, **PTP** has a **timestamp** and a **defined timeline** attached to it! An example might be: Starting today October 1st, 2017, I will lose twenty pounds by March 28th 2018. A time stamp and timeline <u>must be attached</u> and **written down**! As you remember from The Time Factor Chapter 22, **If it's worth living, It's worth writing down.** Writing things down, having an official timestamp, and a timeline is the key for the completion of a goal or mission you have. If no finish line is attached, most likely, the goal will wind up in the *lost-and-found department of the universe of unsaved intellectual property.* Let's just say the odds of it getting done at all, or getting done in a timely manner, has been drastically diminished. *So* **write** *the goal, the start and a finish date* **down**, and apply the *PowerTime Plus* formula: **daily minutes** x **focused action** = **PTP (dm x fa**=PTP). The great thing about PTP is that you don't have to *spend hours* of your "free time" to get those *longer-range goals* done! You just have to be able to repeat the <u>daily focused action over time</u> and let the compounding effect do its thing! If you have sixty-minutes to work out, that's what you do for those 3,600 seconds... **work out!** *No phones,* *texts, email, TV, and no other interruptions please...* **This is PTP** and **PTP** has **NO TIME** for **shenanigans.** You are either in **PTP** or you're **NOT**! There are no fifty shades of gray here. Remember *effortful control* from The Time Factor book? If not, revisit it or look it up on Google.

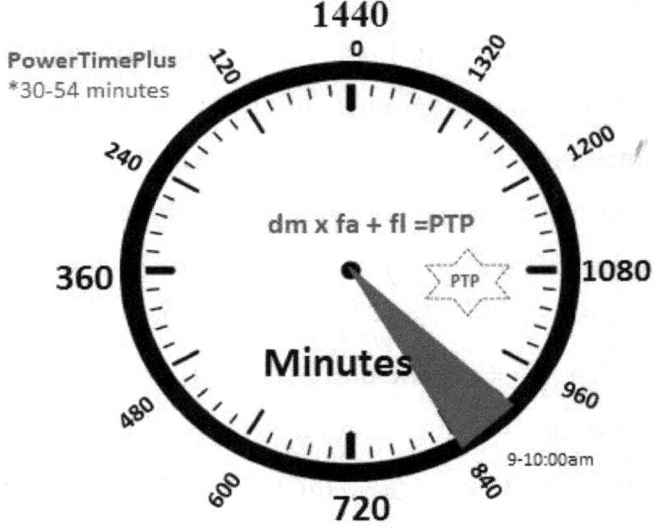

http://www.child-encyclopedia.com/temperament/according-experts/temperamental-effortful-control-self-regulation

You have 300-540 minutes a day when in **ON-TIME,** that is... when you are not sleeping or working at your JOB. You only need **10%** of your **OT** for **PTP,** or in the example above that's 30 to 54 minutes a day over weeks or months to get those longer-range goals completed!

59

Let's recap:

Sleep time is for repairing the cells and resting the mind & body to function at peak performance for the 1020-1080 **waking minutes** we have each day.
*Just cutting back from seven-and-a-half to six-and-a-half hours' sleep a night, genes that are associated with processes like inflammation, immune response, cancer, diabetes, and response to stress became more active.

Work time is for *making money* and the company or entity usually owns this space time. Using the 1440PS here is great for company productivity, but maybe not as good for you... if being paid hourly. However, if someone had to be fired, it might not be you. If your job is what you truly love, or you're making a livelihood doing what you're passionate about, use PT and PTP here. You'll get even more work done in less time.

On-Time is <u>your time</u>. Even though some of it is fixed, such as appointments, children, chores etc., it's yours, not the companies. Free choice reigns here. *It is the only time in which you have to go for more, physically, educationally, or monetarily,* if you so choose.

Genius begins great works; labor alone finishes them.
—Joseph Joubert

Minute Thinking

Just say "NO" to the hour! It has been used on the old-time clock for centuries and must immediately be retired. Don't be an old timer unless you happen to be going to Old Timer's Day at Yankee Stadium and your name is Buddy Brown. We already think in minutes many times throughout the day and most mornings! Your brain is very good at it when it needs to be. **1440TIME™** uses the minute system most effectively in *On-Time* because this is **"your time"**. By breaking down the clock into minutes, the brain will calculate how much time an event will approximately take, e.g., *the laundry (20mins), cutting the lawn (45mins), taking your daughter to dance (15 mins each way), or grocery shopping (60 mins).* You would still have 340 minutes in this example before you would enter *sleep zone* using eight hours (480 minutes) for *On-Time*. That is still plenty of time to go for more. The cool thing is, you will be able to wear 1440TIME™ on your wrist or get the app soon to keep you in check all throughout you On-Time zone!

Be quick, don't hurry. — John Wooden

If you don't have "much time" during your normal work week, it will be **your weekends** when "time optimization" is paramount. Each weekend is two complete days comprised of about **two thousand waking minutes**, give or take a few, depending on your sleep time. If you multiply two thousand by fifty-two weeks per year, that's over *100,000 minutes*—the equivalent in time to about six to eight years of a college education—a Masters or a PhD degree.

The point is, if your work weeks are tough on time, <u>use some weekend minutes to catch up to go for more</u>. A weekend might look like this using The 1440 Power System®:

Free minutes on weekends = 1,920

- o   Eight hours for sleep
- o   Sixteen for waking hours: (16 x 60x 2 = 1,920)

<u>1920 x 52 = 99,948 total minutes in year!</u>

In times of change the learners inherit the earth, while the learned find themselves beautifully equipped for a world that no longer exists.

—Eric Hofer

Saturday (Saturn's Day) and Sunday (Sun's Day) are words that have developed meanings of their own. They are now synonymous with "off" days or "do what I want" days for most. They are just another 1,440 minutes!

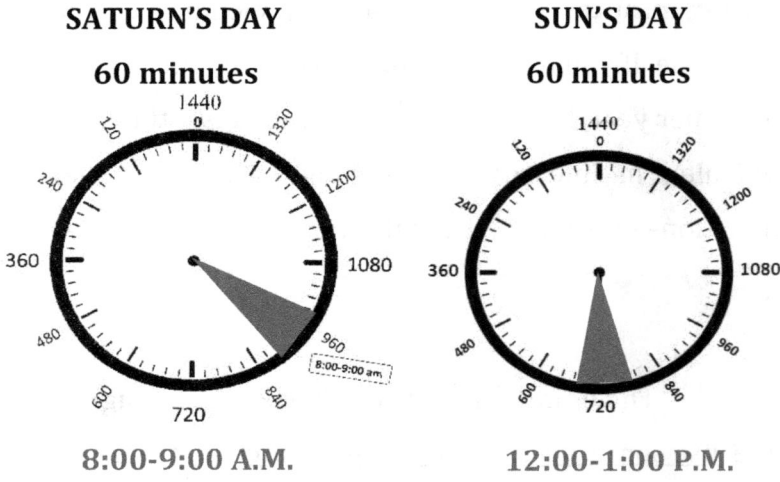

SATURN'S DAY	**SUN'S DAY**
60 minutes	**60 minutes**
8:00-9:00 A.M.	12:00-1:00 P.M.

When we apply PT and **PTP** on the weekends, we hit a grand slam! You know if you want more in your life, *e.g., better fitness, become smarter, and maybe make more money*, you must **pay yourself first** with **time,** and what better time than the weekend to do it? Just sixty **PTP minutes** out of the 960 minutes of waking time you have (*using 8 hours for sleep*) still leaves you **900 hundred minutes** to cut the grass, go to the beach, food shop, seek spiritual pursuits, enjoy parties, go to the mall, or watch a sporting event, and if you're in **PT** mode, you're rockin'. While millions live their weekends unconsciously being controlled by its brevity and ancient meaning (**OFF**) you have plenty (**ON**)—consciously enjoying your *two thousand long expanded weekend minutes.*

This simple innovation paradigm shift for the way you experience your weekend time is all you need if you really want to go for more in your life. Using The 1440 Power System® to have "more" time on weekends feels good—*you have paid yourself first* and still get to enjoy the *weekend* like everyone else. I know just 120 minutes in one weekend won't make you Kevin O'Leary, a Ph.D.., or an Olympic athlete, but over fifty two weeks, that small amount of **PTP** adds up to over *6,200 power minutes* in one year, the equivalent in time to about **two and a half full college courses**. Moreover, when applying the compounding effect of **PTP**, you could be quite smart in most any topic you choose in 3-6 months! And, if any of that time were utilized for fitness, you certainly would be healthier and in better shape than you are now!

Time and I against any two. — Baltasar Gracian

Quick note on the Compound Value of Time (CVT)

CVT works off the same principle the Time Value of Money has in investment theory, and how the power of compounding interest works over time.

"Compound interest is the eighth wonder of the world. He who understands it, earns it... He who doesn't, pays it"... attributed to Albert Einstein

The more I've looked at the Time Value of Money principle over my years in finance, the more it became clear: Replace the word **"money"** with **"time"** and you get the **"Time Value"** of **"Time"**.
He, who understands it, earns it...He who doesn't, pays it...

What is the Time value of money?

The time value of **money** is **money's** potential to grow in value over time. Because of this **potential**, money that's available in the present is considered more valuable than the same amount in the future.
Source: free dictionary.com

Arguing with a fool only proves there are two.
— Doris M. Smith

65

Now replace the word **money and moneys** with time!

The time value of **time** is **time's** potential to grow in value over time. Because of this **potential**, TIME that's available in the present is considered more valuable than the same amount in the future. *Source: Kevin McGrane*

So, invest some **daily minutes** (present value) in any goal or worthy ideal, and those minutes will grow in value over time (future value). ***What a concept...***

PowerTime Plus (PTP) Formula: *daily minutes x focused action =* ***PTP*** *(dm x fa =PTP).*

Let's sum it up like this. If you want more money, you either spend some of your **On-Time minutes** working a *part-time job* or something that could bring you more money down the road, e.g., higher or financial education, or an idea for a better mouse trap to sell, **or you do not.** Such is life...

'Time is money,' says the proverb, but turn it around and you get a precious truth: Money is time.
— George Gissing

Final Notes:

Focus on Your Game...The Best Game in Town!

So many people waste time and energy on things that are meaningless, or over things they have little or no control. They sabotage their own game and wonder why things are not clicking, and haven't been clicking for a while. Think about this: What does your sports team winning or losing have to do with *your physical fitness*? What does Hollywood have to do *with you reading more books*? What do the financial scandals have to do *with you learning about investing*? What does Facebook have to do *with you using the Internet as a powerful tool for self-education?* The decline of the stock market, who became President, a bad economy, or the past, are still not valid reasons why we can't prosper and thrive in this world of technological abundance at our fingertips instantaneously. Are we doing what we should be doing every day to live a prosperous and healthy life in this phenomenal age in time?

Never contend with a man who has nothing to lose.
— Baltasar Gracian

You are never too old:

"I am off to dance lessons ..."

At age 86:
Katherine Pelton swam the 200-meter butterfly in 3 minutes, 1.14 seconds, beating the men's world record for the 85-to-89 age group by over 20 seconds.
At age 88:
Michelangelo created the architectural plans for the Church of Santa Maria degli Angeli.
At age 90:
Pablo Picasso was still producing drawings and engravings.
At age 92:
Paul Spangler finished his fourteenth marathon.
At age 95:
Nola Ochs became the oldest person to receive a college diploma, a degree in general studies with an emphasis on history.
At age 101:
Mary Hardison, 101, became the oldest woman to do a tandem paraglide.

You are never too old to set another goal or to dream a new dream. — C.S. Lewis

Resources:

Why is Sleep Important?

Source: http://www.prevention.com/health/health-concerns/sleep-center/why-sleep-so-important

Importance of Sleep: Six reasons not to scrimp on sleep

Source: http://www.health.harvard.edu/press_releases/8-tips-to-a-good-nights-sleep-without-medicine-from-the-harvard-womens-health-watch

Lack of sleep

http://living.msn.com/style-beauty/makeup-skin-care-hair-tips/10-surprising-things-that-are-aging-you-1#7

Deep Sleep Now By Dr. Oz and Dr. Michael Roizen

Source: http://www.oprah.com/health/Deep-Sleep-Now-Staying-Young/1

A History of Timekeeping

http://timekeepingsite.org/

Calendars through the Ages

http://www.webexhibits.org/calendars/week.html

September, Formerly the Seventh Month of the Roman calendar

History of the Calendar

http://www.infoplease.com/ipa/A0002061.html

Ancient Mythology of The Calendar

http://www.squidoo.com/ancient-myths-calendar

*Calendar September, October, November, December Names of

months in Latin http://wordinfo.info/unit/3197

The seven-day week comes from the seven most visible planets to man long ago—the Sun, Moon, Mercury, Venus, Mars, Saturn and Jupiter? Wikipedia Encyclopedia
The word calendar is derived from the Latin *calendarium*, meaning an interest or account book, and is related to the Latin word *kalend*, meaning "I cry!" (From *The Origins of Our Modern Calendar* by Linda Kerr). Debts were due and these books kept track of who paid and owed.

We don't read books
1/3 of high school graduates never read another book for the rest of their lives.
42 percent of college graduates never read another book after college.
80 percent of U.S. families did not buy or read a book last year.
http://bookstatistics.com/

Time Spent Watching TV
http://adage.com/article/mediaworks/time-spent-watching-tv/227022/

Let's recap: Sleep
*http://www.bbc.co.uk/news/magazine-24444634

Things Other People Accomplished
When They Were Your Age
http://www.museumofconceptualart.com/accomplished/

Quotes from
Brainyquotes.com, quotationsbook.com, thinkexist.com

worldofquotes.com, goodreads.com

```
1388    1388    1388    1388
1398   SYSTEM RESTORED   1398
1408    1408    1408    1408
1418    1418    1418    1418
1428    1428    1428    1428
1438    1438    1438    1438
```

The 1440 Power System®
1440TIME™

We have been socially conditioned over eons to think of time as words on a calendar and numbers on a clock. Readers will learn that the calendars and clocks developed centuries ago are not effective for today's speed of life. We've been trained to act in a certain way, often in conflict with the best use of our time. We underestimate the power of thoughts and words, and how it affects our progress. By the positive redirection and rethinking of our beliefs and the way we view the clock, **time itself becomes a powerful and potent tool to build an extraordinary life on your terms.** Whether you're trying to make more money, lose weight, pick up a new hobby, go back to school, finish that latest best-selling book, or simply create more time in your day, The 1440 Power System® delivers the real deal...

> **1440TIME™**
> **Long Island, NY**
> Phone (631) 946-8811
> www.1440time.com
> 1440time@gmail.com
> twitter@timemaster1440

www.ingramcontent.com/pod-product-compliance
Lightning Source LLC
Chambersburg PA
CBHW060705030426
42337CB00017B/2771